Walking Stick

Monica Harris

Heinemann Library
Chicago, Illinois

Designed by Ginkgo Creative, Inc.
Printed in China.
Photo research by Scott Braut

07 06
10 9 8 7 6 5 4 3

Library of Congress Cataloging-in-Publication Data
Harris, Monica, 1964-
  Walking stick / Monica Harris.
    p. cm. — (Bug books)
Summary: Describes the physical characteristics, habitat, behavior, and life cycle of the insect called the walking stick.
Includes bibliographical references (p.   ).
  ISBN: 1-40340-766-5 (HC), 1-40340-995-1 (Pbk.)
  1. Stick insects—Juvenile literature. [1. Stick insects.] I. Title.
II. Series.
  QL509.5 .H37 2003
  595.7'29—dc21
                                    2002004028

Acknowledgments
The author and publishers are grateful to the following for permission to reproduce copyright material:
pp. 4, 8 E. A. Janes/NHPA; pp. 5, 27 James H. Robinson; p. 6 Buddy Mays/Corbis; p. 7 Michael Fogden/Oxford Scientific Films; p. 9 Kjell Sandved; p. 10 Nuridsany et Perennou/Photo Researchers, Inc.; p. 11 Gregory G. Dimijian/Photo Researchers, Inc.; p. 12 Ann & Rob Simpson; p. 13 Anthony Bannister/Gallo Images/Corbis; p. 14 David Fox/Oxford Scientific Films; p. 15 James Soloman/USDA Forest Service/www.forestryimages.org; p. 16 John Shaw/Bruce Coleman Inc.; pp. 17, 23, 28 Dr. James L. Castner; p. 18 Brian Sytnyk/MasterFile; pp. 19, 20 Mantis Wildlife Films/Oxford Scientific Films; p. 21 Ray Coleman/Photo Researchers, Inc.; p. 22 Gerald & Buff Corsi/Visuals Unlimited; p. 24 William E. Ferguson; p. 25 P. Ormay/Australian National Botanic Gardens; p. 26 Jeff J. Daly/Visuals Unlimited; p. 29 Breck P. Kent/JLM Visuals.

Illustration, p. 30, by Will Hobbs.
Cover photograph by Rick C. West.

Every effort has been made to contact copyright holders of any material reproduced in this book. Any omissions will be rectified in subsequent printings if notice is given to the publisher.

Special thanks to Dr. William Shear, Department of Biology, Hampden-Sydney College, for his review of this book.

Some words are shown in bold, **like this**. You can find out what they mean by looking in the glossary.

Contents

What Are Walking Sticks?

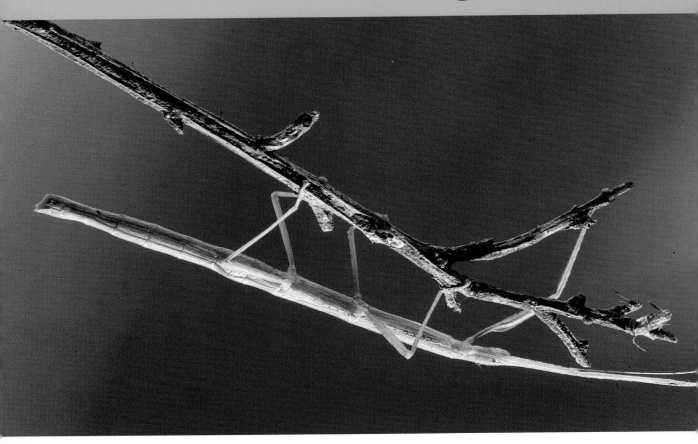

Walking sticks are **insects.** They have six legs, two eyes, and two **antennae.** Some have two wings. Most walking sticks look just like sticks.

Walking sticks come in many colors and shapes. They can be brown, gray, tan, or green. Walking sticks live in trees or bushes. They can be very hard to see.

What Do Walking Sticks Look Like?

Walking stick bodies have a head, a **thorax,** and an **abdomen.** Their legs look like thin twigs on a branch. Even their **antennae** look like twigs.

Walking sticks look like the plants they live on. This is called **mimicry.** Their body parts may look like leaf buds. This walking stick looks like the moss plant it is sitting on.

How Big Are Walking Sticks?

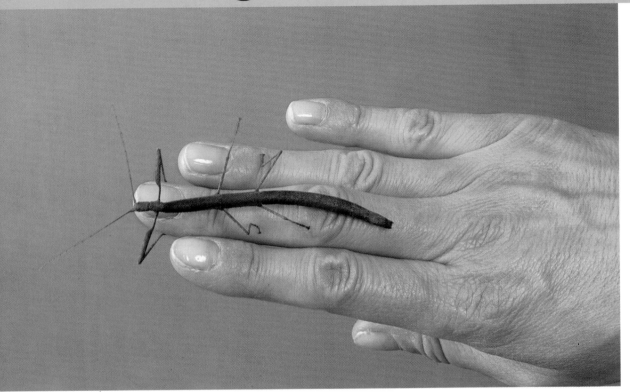

Most walking sticks would fit in the palm of your hand.

Some walking sticks are very large. When they stretch their front legs forward, they may look two times as long. **Females** are often bigger than **males.**

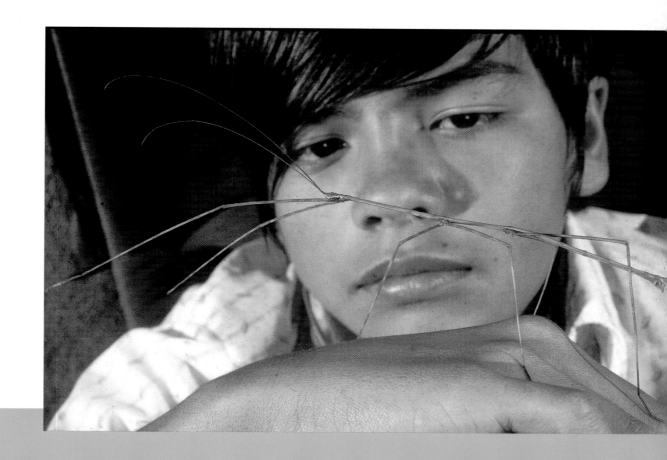

How Are Walking Sticks Born?

Females lay from 100 to 1,300 eggs in the spring. The eggs usually fall to the ground. Some walking sticks put their eggs under the dirt or stick them to leaves. The eggs look like plant seeds.

Nymphs hatch in three to eighteen months. Nymphs look like little **adults.** One nymph could fit on your fingertip.

How Do Walking Sticks Grow?

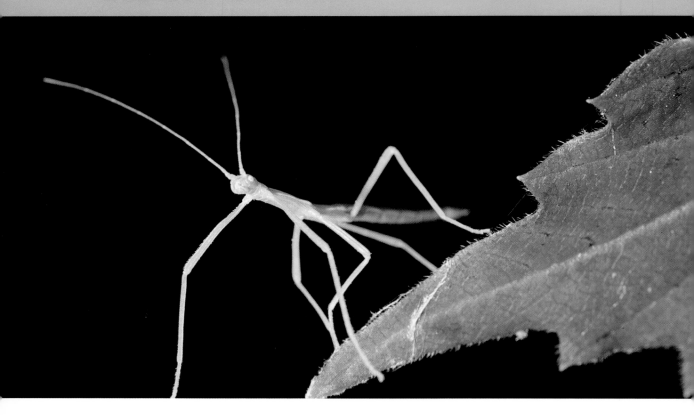

As **nymphs** grow, their skin becomes too small. They shed it for a new skin. This is called **molting.** The new skin is bigger and sometimes darker.

Nymphs become **adults** in three to twelve months. **Males** molt five times. Adult males have wings. **Females** molt six times. Only a few females have wings.

What Do Walking Sticks Eat?

Walking sticks are **herbivores,** or plant eaters. They have strong jaws to cut and chew leaves. They usually eat at night.

Sometimes, there are too many walking sticks. They eat so many leaves that it hurts the trees. This walking stick ate most of these leaves.

Which Animals Attack Walking Sticks?

Birds, spiders, mice, lizards, and other insects eat walking sticks. Walking sticks fall to the ground to **protect** themselves. They pull their legs in and don't move.

Some walking sticks spray a stinky liquid from their **thorax.** It burns the eyes and skin of the **predator.** A few walking sticks can change colors.

Where Do Walking Sticks Live?

Walking sticks live where it is warm. They live in grasslands, **temperate forests,** and **tropical** places. All walking sticks live on plants.

Walking sticks do not build homes or nests. They spend most of their time walking on tree branches. They even **molt** there.

How Do Walking Sticks Move?

Walking sticks have special claws at the end of their legs. They help the walking stick to hang on. Walking sticks can even hang upside down.

Walking sticks move very slowly. This makes them hard to see. Some walking sticks rock from side to side. They **mimic** a branch moving in the breeze.

How Long Do Walking Sticks Live?

Most walking sticks live about one year. Large walking sticks can live longer. It takes them longer to grow. They may live up to two years.

Some walking sticks have bright colors. The colors might tell **predators** to stay away. These walking sticks might live longer!

What Do Walking Sticks Do?

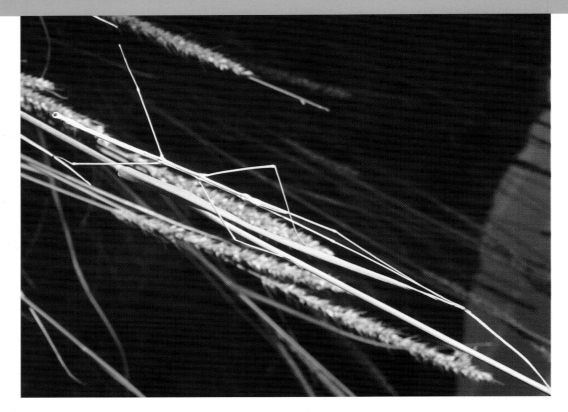

Walking sticks use **mimicry.** They look like something else. Walking sticks look like twigs.

Walking sticks eat plants. They ate a piece of this leaf. Walking sticks can harm a forest if there are too many of them.

How Are Walking Sticks Special?

Walking sticks have an escape trick. If a **predator** grabs their leg, the leg breaks off. This walking stick lost a leg to a predator.

Walking sticks can **regenerate** body parts. This means they can grow new body parts. When the walking stick **molted,** it grew back its lost leg.

Thinking about Walking Sticks

Can you find the walking stick? Why is it so hard to find?

Even walking stick eggs are hard to find. What do these eggs look like?

Walking Stick Map

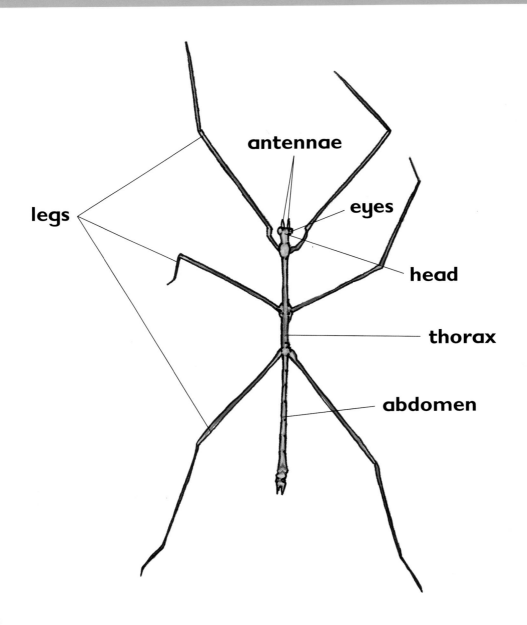

antennae

legs

eyes

head

thorax

abdomen

Glossary

abdomen belly of an animal

adult grown-up

antennae (one is an **antenna**) body parts that sense touch and smell

female girl

hatch come out of an egg

herbivore animal that eats plants

insect animal with six legs and three body parts

male boy

mimic look or act like something else

mimicry looking or acting like something else

molt get rid of skin that is too small

nymph baby walking stick

predator animal that hunts other animals for food

protect keep safe

regenerate to make a new body part

temperate forests forest in a place where there are four seasons

thorax chest of an insect's body

tropical warm

More Books to Read

Paige, Joy. *The Stick Insect: World's Longest Insect.* New York: PowerKids Press, 2002.

Green, Tamara. *Walking Sticks.* Milwaukee, Wisc.: Gareth Stevens, 1997.

Index